Your Perfect Lips

A Spiritual-Erotic Memoir

Stuart Sovatsky

For Sultana
Wanted, craved to
be with
love

iUniverse, Inc.
New York Lincoln Shanghai

Your Perfect Lips
A Spiritual-Erotic Memoir

iUniverse books may be ordered through booksellers or by contacting:

iUniverse
2021 Pine Lake Road, Suite 100
Lincoln, NE 68512
www.iuniverse.com
1-800-Authors (1-800-288-4677)

ISBN-13: 978-0-595-37587-5 (pbk)
ISBN-13: 978-0-595-81982-9 (ebk)
ISBN-10: 0-595-37587-1 (pbk)
ISBN-10: 0-595-81982-6 (ebk)

Printed in the United States of America

Your Perfect Lips

Moreover, we need to consider the possibility that one day, perhaps, in a different economy of bodies and pleasures, people will no longer quite understand how the ruses of sexuality, and the power that sustains its organization, were able to subject us to that austere monarchy of sex, so that we became dedicated to the endless task of forcing its secret, of exacting the truest of confessions from a shadow.

The irony of this deployment [of modern sexuality] *is in having us believe that our* "*liberation*" [by its ways alone] *is in the balance.*
(Michel Foucault, *The History of Sexuality*, final words)

Where man and woman worship one another
is the play of the divine.
Tantra Shastras

Contents

ONE

I never felt so all alone from the rest of the world
and totally with another person
as when I first undressed you incredible
and you me slowly deliberately unbelievable
in your low-ceilinged bedroom pressed up against
the edge of your bed after that time, our second, of kissing.
Remember that day? When we first got together to "talk?"
Intrigued over the years with fleeting conversations
about other things like India or motorcycles
and those vaguely-met gazes,
we curiously or perhaps inevitably
approached each other the night before
about this and that and somebody who had died
who knew something
and so you asked me what I knew about it,
a "way" or whatever where every thought act moment counts
and thus is purported to contain everything, centermost,
a rare kind of sex perhaps as endless as it is imaginary
in which the goal of gendered human existence awaits,
a bliss enhanced with unbearable longing and hungers
and thus as foreboding as it is alluring,
perhaps a little dangerous,
but maybe moreso to live without ever trying.

So you came over to talk, your scarf in the wind,
I let you in my door and a few minutes later
there you were sitting across from me,
beautiful and shy and listening for real
so how could I not become enthralled with you,
the very subject of my words,
worshipful and in awe of you,
woman that you are—
so all this led up to the next moment
and all else rushed forth after that
saturating the minutes days months ahead
with us running trying stumbling to catch up.

It was in that moment that I became
quite suddenly enchanted by your throat,
there, in the silky crevice
where fleeting shadows hover so hauntingly
where your breath rises and then vanishes—
that I decided to, to, touch you there
all the while explaining to you
that I was being drawn to doing this to you
as a kind of devotion, a holy act,
something I have seen children do
when they try to touch a butterfly
without causing it to fly away,
they reach without noticing
they have stopped breathing,
holding their breaths,

out of the strange wonder they feel
for the velvety-winged creature,
as if it were another sort of child
more beautiful than themselves,
like how they stand before a newborn,
leaning backward, turning on one foot,
slightly over-powered by the newborn's slowly whirring vortex,
the child stands sideways spellbound
at the mystery there before him,
his eyes brimming remembering,
vaguely dislodged, from somewhere else—

And of course all that trails backward in time
to the very first moment I ever laid eyes on you,
before I touched your satiny throat the mystery of your life,
and had then slowly kissed your lips perfect lips,
yes before that three years before
when you first ever entered my field of vision
at that art opening basement-like,
with the maroon walls pinioned with large-framed little paintings
of harlequins and mimes & gauze weavings strewn through
with seaweed strands holding a doll's arm
or a watch or drooping feathers,
you walked from that other dimly-lit room
toward me in this room
unusually close to your boyfriend at the time.

Wow. I hoped no one heard me, it was that loud in my head.
Then envy then wow unbelievable not likely no way just let it go
say Hi, you say Hi, he says Hi, Hi and then everybody washes past
into the oblivion of that crowded evening
of countless such evenings
quickened pulses that wash away
making cliff-sides into sand grains then dust flecks
that float upwards sideways glittering from a certain angle,
drifting into the airless black night moon and stars.

In between, for those three years,
in the ultimacy or nothingness of duration-spent,
perhaps a secret future connected us.
Or even before that in the space between your birth and mine,
almost a decade,
with the location of yours just a few hours from my Mother's,
how odd, or rather, how perfect or silly to think on it.
Such is the power of narrative, this way or that way
words seduce convince jerk us about,
this adjective that adverb making more or less of events or nonevents
or those missed like the second largest ritual gathering on the planet
that almost no one here knows about,
continuous for several thousand years mid-summer
with three million revelers last count who amassed at Puri, India
for *Ratha-Yatra*, the Chariot Festival,
where a tiny wide-eyed Lord *Krishna* idol Reality
sits with his tiny beloved *Radha* idol Reality
atop a sixty-five-ton wooden chariot,
three stories high,
with eight wheels on either side,
intentionally carved *un*-even
so as to make the behemoth lurch
unpredictably, teeter to an ominous halt,
then, rocking mysteriously,

it re-gains momentum careening down the winding Puri streets
barely holding itself together
like human lives themselves
like the Universe itself
continuing on and on for three days
provoking the throngs to pray or cheer in awe or terror
or hurl insults at *Krishna* their Beloved
with the elusive sexual past,
deepening their intimacy with Him and His Beloved *Radha*
while not too long ago a desperate few
would get completely frenzied
and hurl themselves beneath the grinding wheels
expecting *maha-samadhi, moksha,* highest liberation
instantaneously.

All the while *Krishna* as *Jagannatha* "Lord of the Universe"
is merely relentlessly unfolding moment-to-moment
this very indeterminate and wavery universe,
three-quarters dark and invisible to us
(as physicists concurred 5000 years later),
one-quarter bright seen mercurial.
His wide-eyed-look alongside the Beloved *Radha's*
the selfsame look in two different-gendered bodies
also peering out of your mind eyes ears tongue skin,
mine, all minds bodies yet and ever alive,
but only always right-NOW-NOW-NOW
(as you read this, *that* racing-forth chariot)

the past receding ribbonlike
flailing into oblivion,
as everything just keeps racing forward
with every word choice action this way,
word choice action that way,
whole universes of possibilities come to the verge
and then wash into another
as time keeps catapulting everything forward,
as the English-derived term, juggernaut, conveys.

But, get into the perfectly romantic narrative
and languidly attuned gaze
and what reveals itself
is the sheer poignancy poetry wonder of
the relentless never-happened-before-always
—*Sanatana Dharma*, The Eternal Ordering-Way—
shimmering with hopes and hints of a divine passion
that nourishes forgives matures each being
toward an evermore enlightened version of itself.
Awaiting your devotion,
hovering just beneath the surface,
outside of all lesser narratives myths possibilities
and the fallen world that results inexorably
from repeated listening to acting on them
and repeated dismissing yea fearing
the romantic hope.

That *a-dharmic* world is with us now:
A barely sustainable broken place
the ancient forest-dwellers 10,000 years ago warned of
with its roots growing too much down
and not enough up, or the reverse,
leaving the mercurial romance of reality
to atrophy into a dreaminess or barren cynicism.
Broken relationships marriages homes lives.

That is the world in which we meet,
where romance is no longer the one thing
nor gender worship continuous and strong
a hundred generations back, the way without a second
the very air we breathe.
But no matter, awake and above the fray,
in their eternal romance are *Radha* and *Krishna*
and each one of us is *Radha* and *Krishna*.

Imagine an alternative Christ
whose message of love and redemption is conveyed,
not by a story of heroic self-sacrifice and martyrdom,
but by the passionate love between Man and Woman,
the Perfected Couple as Religion,
a Mystico-Erotica as its most sacred scripture.
As *Krishna* proclaimed of Himself in his *Song of God,*
"I am the *passion* in beings that is attuned to [*Sanatana*] *Dharma.*"
A rare kind of sex
in which desire shudders throughout the body
in myriad crescendos of awe heat and bliss
rendering all bodiless religions and myopic sexologies
vestigial to an age on the wane
that had become dedicated to exacting the truest of confessions
from a shadow.

How so?

Far beyond the thrall of the teenaged awakening
Nature has hidden in us
numerous rare and mysterious erotic reflexes
and transformative puberties
(except for "Kundalini," completely unknown to modern times—
did we really believe we had discovered
everything there is about the erotic universe?)
the fleshy basis of all spiritual yearning
that only an ever-deeper passion might awaken:
Shuddering genital reversals *vajroli mudra, shakti chalani,*
that emerge in meditative depths
or only after the second hour of embrace,
spinal surges *Kundalini-shakti, davvening,*
Quakering, Shakering, zikr-ing, holy ghosting,
involving perhaps twenty year novitiates of sublimative maturation,
excessively devotional surrenders
requiring an ease with tears
at the thought of it all,
and even more distant throat-choking pharyngeal hypoglossal arousals
khecari mudra,

soaring into consummate pineal emissions
soma-rasa, nectar of the gods,
inebriating the inmost soul
with breathless beauties everywhere,
perhaps a dozen lifetimes away.
In a different economy of bodies and pleasures
we might call these awakenings postgenital puberties
as in the ancient name for Yoga: *shamanica medhra,*
"the going-beyond-genital-awakenings"
—but beyond into *what?*

Always oscillating, *Krishna* worships *Radha* worships *Krishna*
man worships woman worships man
thus becoming god, becoming goddess
from the inside out molting their human skins
born out of their arduous longing for this other, the beloved,
the ache of it all endured,
this life into That into this into That,
a weaving maturing of souls verging on oneness,
circling auguring ever-deeper
into the Source of incarnation itself,
close and even closer
winding toward the vertiginous center
everything quickening the hopes and fears
of each lover there ever was or will be.

Stuart Sovatsky

The awe of creation, the power of it, life itself.
Immortality inward outward the other puberties
endlessly beyond words English or Sanskrit to this edge
Where Happening itself happens this miracle then this,
in which we guide word choice action toward that
purr in your voice that breaks into sighs
hand gripped onto your pelvis breaking free no end can be seen.

The romantic narrative begins easily:
Your eyes, my wonder, your lips, my hunger,
your wisdom, my mystery.
I love you yes till death do us yes and yes again yes
yes the only word I know
that dusky taste of your interior thigh
my forever and ever.
I will never leave you
for where else is there to go?

Devouring each other upward, however,
from the spinal tree of knowledge, of life, *elan vital* itself,
becomes the (secret) maturational pathway
for the evermore incarnating spirit—
From one branch serving as fulcrum to the next
all the way up from *lingam* and *yoni*
to the crown the radiant jewel the conduit
a river of concentration surging
inward vibrating serpentine *Kundalini-shakti*
backward upward through the violet-tinged perineum *trikonam*
("triangular city of fire, flashing forth like lightning bolts
and resembling molten gold" *Goraksha Paddhati 1.20*)
and up the milky-white spinal cord
into the cranial heaven-realms of erogenous Mind
vaginal-satiny brain flesh
seething sulci thousand-petalled orgasms
beyond the covered in shame garbled tales of *Genesis*
all the way up to drink the pineal *soma-rasa*
nectar of the gods alchemical elixir, heady froth
au—mmmmmmmnnnn.... **Shivaaaaha-a-a**!
Delirious, you called it, I give up, you sighed.

Stuart Sovatsky

Therein quickens the final the pineal puberty
seat of the soul with glimmering signs everywhere
Hopi Kahuna Inuit Santeria Andalusian Romani
Masonic Oneidan Aboriginal Yoruban Celtic
Confucian Jain Sikh Siberian Sufi Charismatic
Tantric Bhakti Carmelite Carthusian Franciscan
Jesuit Camaldolese Capucian Brigittine Bon
Dzogchen Taoist Tibetan gTummo/Chandal
Saivite Buddhist Zoroastrian Gnostic Mithraic
Coptic Cartesian Egyptian Kabbalism Eleusinian
Platonic Christian—
When thine eyes become single
there will be no more [ordinary] male or female—
hypothalamic polypeptides age-reversing melatonin
ecstasy-inducing endorphin, dimethyl triptamine
take me, take me, always your last words.

The most well-known advanced aspects
of primordial gender worship
have occurred internally within the person of a singular body
surrendering alone to the longings
attaining *samadhi* realization, the end of longing.
Let's face it, it's simpler to go farther alone.
One other person adds a universe of differences to work out—
worship and the awe of gender, the purpose of it all—
ironically, tragically, over and over again,
get lost in the tussle, in the overgrown artifice of "worldly life"—or worse.

But who can know for sure,
did the solo travelers manifest the complete *dharma*?
Even so, the path of extraordinary pairs
taking their longing elsewhere has left few traces.
Beyond the reach of simple blasphemy or happy desires
into the realms of pure risk adventures beyond the pale
based in profundity lived prized shared as sacred trust
the undeniable persisting superlative consensus of two people.
Would that be you and me?

In a different economy of bodies and pleasures
each couple a universe unto themselves,
sheltering their children, grand- and great-grand-children
in expanding overlapping bio-radiant fields of gender worship,
all growing magnificently in love and awe.
Ten-thousand couples become a *sangha* community,
ten-thousand *sanghas* a *pradesh* state,
ten-thousand states a *loka* realm,
ten realms the world, *Vasudaiva kutumbakam*—
The world is, indeed, one family.
One billion vibrant planetary households,
sacred *grihasthya,* the center that holds each and all
the lion with the lamb
the endless wedding feast
gender worship on high
manifested on earth as it is in heaven.
Throw open the secret passage:

In the [secret] erotic art, truth is drawn from pleasure itself,
understood as a practice and accumulated as experience;
pleasure is not considered in relation to an absolute law of
the permitted and the forbidden, nor by reference to a
criterion of utility, but first and foremost in relation to itself,
it is experienced as pleasure, evaluated in terms of its intensity,
its specific quality, its duration, its reverberations in the body
and the soul. Moreover, this knowledge must be deflected back
into the sexual practice itself, in order to shape it as though from
within and amplify its effects. In this way, there is formed a
knowledge that must remain secret, not because of an element
of infamy that might attach to its object, but because of the need
to hold it in the greatest reserve, since according to the tradition,
it would lose its effectiveness and its virtue by being divulged....
The effects of this masterful art, which are considerably more
generous than the spareness of its prescriptions would lead one
to imagine, are said to transfigure the one fortunate enough to
receive its privileges: an absolute mastery of the body, a singular bliss,
obliviousness to time and limits, the elixir of life, the exile of death
and its threats.

(Foucault, *The History of Sexuality*, NY: Vintage, 1984, pp. 57-58)

This is the universal way, the wavering *tan-tra* in Sanskrit,
tao-ta in Mongolian, *tao* in Chinese:
"The *Tao* of one-name is inadequate
to the ambiguous two-sided Eternal *Tao*.
In the shimmering in-between
where the mystery is the deepest
is the gateway to all that is subtle and wonderful."
Lao-tse *Tao the Ching* (Ch1-v1)

Stuart Sovatsky

TWO

Most of those first three years
whenever we were in the same room,
I had my eyes closed, wailing away
with our lean didge player baying into a hollowed root
with the synchopating drummers alongside
while crowds danced oblivious as I was to them
lost in my worship of you the longing of my longing.
Almost wordless with hints maybe here and there,
as we later confided in each other.
So you knew me secretly more than I even guessed,
until you told me so.

Then words snapped into hopes to be known
to go to that place together
where the right-and left-handed paths converge.
That is the trail. Our trail, it turns out,
that led three years later to that night, nearly one year ago,
to another different art opening
leather clothing smart drinks Burning-man videos,
when you came up to me with your question.
Somebody had died, the boyfriend was over and I answered yes,
of course, we could talk about that
but was that a veil, destiny, or was it a dream I had?
The words yes, the heat yes,
but what connected them altogether?
Something, us maybe yes.

It was just the next day after the recent art opening
with the leather the smart the questions,
violet-tinged and enthusiastic you came over
scarf trailing to talk and ask.
Nothing had happened yet on that first day
sharing about devotional love
the everlasting necessary
to provoke those other puberties
unleashing those other passions
beyond sex beyond the world just we two forever.
So how could I not touch your satiny throat
an arm's length away?

Yet in doing so you started to cry as if alone
then looking up leaning into the mystery unfolding
that first slow kiss kissing the selfsame kiss except
one is male the other female kisses the one the other
you me, me you with the verb implied,
that close.

Right then I decided to decide that I knew that I knew.
The pressing equally you toward me me toward you
no-difference a oneness evoking yes
the rest of my life, this is it.
And, thus, rolling over supine onto
the carpet onto you happened
into there here here. But stopping, however,
just in time, you said then but later recanted,
not, it had happened, hadn't had hadn't
something happened, no, something *else* new
not-that but like it portending another
secret behind another and another
upward left-handed *vajroli* sucking backward
urdhva-retas flashing into the spine the hidden mountainous pathway
Meru Carmel Olympus Tree of Knowledge *davvening* into each
other, *zikr*-ing holy ghosting Shaker-shaking Quaker-quaking,
Flamenco's Indic origins, Bushman's ecstatic *thxiasi num,*
into those future puberties awaiting us,

turning on one foot,
the other rushing forth picking-up momentum
dangerously hurling ourselves beneath the wheels,
yet less so than to have lived without ever trying.

That was the Tuesday leading up to that Thursday,
the first time ever at your house,
a cottage streaked with green translucent shadows
tucked away completely hidden behind another streetside-house
accessed by a narrow-passageway low dark
opening into a courtyard garden tended and wild,
up to your porch stuff-stacked hanging plants herbs,
then your many window-paned door.
I knocked wondering alive shaky.
You opened warm. I entered we looked
beginning where we had left off
the heat of it.
Removing my jacket, I took a longer look:
Dressed in jeans white cotton shirt your long yellow hair
eyes as blue-green as mine.
Hi, Hi, come in here.

I recall the kisses of that night especially, so deliberate,
slowly focusing our lips upon one another.
I learned more watching your lips—
so shy and, yet, hopeful, waiting so receptively
as if they were fainting into themselves
into another place far far away—
than your eyes, still tinged with sorrow.
Those lips, wanting more, awaiting more,
this way then that, tongue flicks here and there
then opening into the warm moist cathedral of joined mouths.
That feeling of warm liquified pink,
licking the insides of your cheeks,
beneath your tongue,
drinking each other delicately and then thirstily,
years, decades of thirst coming out.
Pausing, returning, looking hands grazing your breasts
as you leaning leaned further toward me
the tunnel of your deep neckline suddenly dropping down
opening that chasm, the darkness in the center,
your breasts revealed indirectly as you crawled toward me
closing the distance fully desiring whether you knew it or not
for me to see, look, take, please,
reach into me as I reach into you.

And then the sighing emerged the half-unbuttoning
that somehow got in the way
as much as being the way toward one another—
who wants to touch buttons when you are right there?
So, unbuttoning became a slow sacrificial ritual,
the feel of hard pearly plastic being pressed through
dislodging with a tthiiik parts the panels of a shirt blouse
holy ark opens to unseen flesh revealed only for me for you
then slowly tumbling forth a cascade of yeses
you so beautiful in the dim-light
touch here there exquisite reaching down
the tthiiik of waistbands opening and further in
deliberate and pausing, licking here there
the black satin covering slip it down
gradually trapping you for a moment
at the hips thighs knees trapping in exposed shyness
turning away and toward at the same time
like a child velvety-winged provoking tensions
delayed longings and even an uncertainty,
would anything *happen*?

Stuart Sovatsky

Maybe only this far tonight, first night, or this or this,
no, sliding down further toward shyly turned ankles
yours and now mine too,
toward and away,
the slow whirring vortex hushed now
and drops silently to the floor.
You are amazing.
You I come alive to for with are the one
I have been waiting for for so long,
there is no more waiting you said,
here take me you said,
I said now this here oh never so alone
from the rest, with another, ever.

That was the Thursday evening
after the crawling slowly toward
kissing between the two chairs
rising up standing merging feel it? Yes?
Yes and up the turning curve of your stairs, around the landing,
travel things stacked-up,
through the over-sized doorway
into the low-ceilinged bedroom,
you ahead of me now turning around
facing me a little sideways
and me you standing there
with the back of your legs pressed against the edge
shy with anticipation you waited
giving yourself over in a kind of hovering stillness
to my awe of you.

Were you breathing?
It seemed like you were barely
or perhaps holding your breath,
or inhaling very slowly, almost whispering your breath in.
Or was that in response to me
removing your stockings lace bra by degrees pausing,
then another and another.
Were you in awe of me being in awe of you
as I, now, am in awe of the memory of you
seeing me be in awe of you,
me seeing you being in awe of me?
The confusing whirl beyond easy syntax of you and me
becoming u-s us.

I could not believe my eyes.
I must have stopped breathing myself without noticing,
till I would begin again to inhale or release.

To watch someone moment after moment
continuing to find you remarkable
almost as if you are not there to disturb her wonder at you,
calling no attention to yourself,
I watched you discovering me—
the shape of my cheekbones causing this kind of delight,
how my eyes catch the light from a certain angle
stirring you to purse your lips that now become lips
coming toward me to drink my lips for a moment
reflected as you move away finished with that one kiss
in the taste I seem to have left on your lips
in your mind causing heat a wetness
causing suddenly slowly closing of your eyes
and thus mine too
drowning in that dark pool together
where causing comes from.

Your skin was too lovely to touch,
so I was at first reluctant to disturb you.
But you wanted me to disturb you,
to interrupt your separation from me with who I am.
Months later, scores of similar times later,
I am still just waking from my separate dream
to how much you were hoping for me too.
It is not just me. I had to lick, to taste, first.
Then with the lilac taste of you on my lips
savored just a hair-breadth away from your thigh
with my eyes closed you are now on me and I am still tasting you.

With my eyes closed I feel you discovering more of your own beauty
as you feel me savoring you.
In my mind I imagine being in your mind
just as your taste is still on my lips, yours devouring me,
your eyes now oblivious,
you washing forth back like waves along a foamy darkened coastline
everything fading backward receding into the ocean's ever-shifting maw.
As if you had been breathing underwater for a long time,
you look up your face now blurred with drunken passion.
I give up you said. You are torturing me. Take me. Care of me.
Then muffled tears lost fragments of re-arising long-dashed hopes.
You: I am delirious. Me: In a good way, I hope. You: Yes, in a very good way.

With the secret passageway opened backwards and upwards perineal
you could taste and devour all the way up to my mind
so your perfect lips were now *in* my mind
licking the interior darkness billowing responsively in being licked,
licking back your lips carefully reaching into the infinity
with more yearning further further
everywhere we look inwardly, we go on and on
into the dark meringue of sentience echoing in our sighs, archings,
begetting other chained-together sequences of transitive verbs,
each next one the direct object of the last
becomes the subject of the next:
Feeling *feeling* feeling *feeling* taking *giving* taking *giving.*
I regret laundering our sheets, you wrote me the next day,
the sweat of us there the scent lingering
precious fleeting unpredictable.

In the *Vedas* two birds are on a branch,
one eats,
the other watches,
feeding upon the eating one's sheer enjoyment,
who enjoys the watcher's enjoyment of her enjoyed feeding,
adding to the other's adding to.
The memory of it backwards,
the looking forward to it again,
becoming other memories
inspiring other lookings forward
becoming other memories becoming.
Everywhere you look,
then, now, later, feeding or being fed upon,
like the darting beam of a diamond-faceted miner's lamp,
consciousness is *there* and *there* and *there,* a mushrooming infinity of bliss.

Two people chained to one another in endless causality
by their hunger for one another,
irresistibility inciting irresistibility,
chemical fusion reactions of the entire polarized universe.
Every glistening cell poised aiming him her
and nothing else is what every living gendered fiber wants,
has ever wanted
a hundred a thousand a million years
all cresting right now. Feel it.

All verbs nouns perfumes feathers boldness charm
peaking in this moment situated exactly the way
everything in the universe is conspires,
making this happen.
With you, the one who exceeds all expectations
lucky to be with you, lucky to be with *you*.
The *tantra weavedness* of it all,
no longer an Eastern philosophy that includes erotic arts,
but the ineluctable nature of reality—
an intertwining foliating romance, or nothing at all.

Endless amusements. Heshe watches himherself being devoured
proving more nourishing to feel *your joy* in devouring me
than mine received falling backwards supine
but now progressed not onto a floor with serendipitous passion
but in the low-ceilinged bedroom erotic mysteries engaging one another
up the curved stairs,
legs against the edge,
and now falling onto it, it gives-way, cushiony, to our weight.
You looking up, me down,
each mesmerized enthralled exquisite.
Are you happy yes I am happy are you yes I have never been happier.

Stuart Sovatsky

First slowly with kisses everywhere,
the successive hours lost in time
this way then that passage-ways opening
flooding unfurling wrists held down and released
this that um yes and yes
and suddenly you on top at two a.m. there it Is
the frenzy, the shameless unabashed selfish freedom of it all comes out
wild almost hideous the truth of yes wanting mmmmmore,
whispering head turned this way *more*, then that way *more*,
even after the third hour, *more more* and yes of course,
the more you take the better it is,
for here in this endless place, more is all there is.

THREE

Everything was displaced by you that Fall.
Every other sort of hunger left me I lost ten pounds in one week
except that one for you filling every moment asleep awake in-between.
"Filled with joy" is such a ringing singing phrase.
Like shiny brass turquoise and garnet bejeweled Tibetan icon couples
in upright thrilled embrace,
Indian spirituality driven into the mountainous remote
saving itself from uncomprehending desecration
blossomed in those icons secret truths mystico-erotica original religion
fully-matured upward inward all glands alive tumescent engorged
totally intent the one upon the other
perfectly in love
designed by the Cosmos
each quantum crystal species plant animal male and female
to capture the full attention
the one of the other the other of the one
in perfect symmetry.

"Look! Behold! They are like unto gods!"
Unashamed though revealed
and fragile with feelings
like the velvety-wings of a breeze a child turning on one foot
a fawn a leaf quivering.
But also the adult whose complex sensitivities reach out
into the not quite happened yet
dangers and omens
down to the whisper of a lost child any child
yours theirs anywhere anytime search or call,
and equal to dark dark death itself
into which from which All comes and returns.

This is what a man and woman *should be*, you said one morning.
Permission to be
or something even before that,
the *is* of gender itself, *iiizzzzing mmmaallle fffeemmmaallle,*
reaching out through our yearning, seizing limbs
beyond that austere monarchy in a different economy
the entire range of one's embodied nature shoots through,
wind-swaying wildflowers to lonely-baying wolves:
Here, find me calling, waiting, here.

Within "*is*" teems reality, teems gender,
the two matched in every way to meet in the meeting of every surface
merging into here.

We are for ourselves best when we are *for* each other,
a lifelong exploration of the preposition *for*
humble overlooked what are things *for*
a yearning, I am in love with *for,*
giver beyond myself bowing, finally, in devotion
granting exquisiteness to another,
really meaning it,
becoming symbiotic with you, source of my awe.
Orienting the minutes hours toward you,
the purpose to get up early to listen to you breathe,
as the day finally ends racing stop lights to get to you,
greeted by ah nice already unlocked
into the narrow passage
across the moonlit, opening, walking in,
you say when I don't know what else to say I say, *you you*
I say *yes yes.*

Eventually *for* completes itself and extends into *with,*
the primordial pre-position.
Wanted, craved to be *with,* impossible not to,
she flips off her shirt in sudden response to being felt up,
creates an *us,* how far can *with another* be taken?
How far the sustained kiss?
The same breath shared mouth to surrendered mouth,
back and forth, over and over,
higher and higher
exceedingly relaxed exploring etheric realms
now become asphyxiating hungers voraciously aiming
where the life sparks in each other incept
pit of chest, core of brain.

Taking it no more, our minds silently explode with longings electric,
soundlessly shriek, ungrasp the current us
squeeze another us breathless into There—
become a single throbbing thadoom thadoom emerges
the Universal Us swells in grandeur,
lungs stilled, minds now breathing directly into minds,
prana and *citta* scintillate their oneness,
kevala kumbhaka transfixed inspiration
melts us through the fear of breathless death,
vyutthana resurrects Us into another consciousness
then another,
the serene space *vairaghya* dawns,
we collapse gasping amazed.

The softness of your circular *iizziing*
playing in the sand scratches on my back
you humming quietly round and round,
are we ten years old mindlessly drifting
in a spoon-sized infinity?
Or cresting, the distant horizon now visible,
others already passed away, inciting fervor
for what fleeting remains,
my fingernails *iizziizing* down taken over by a storm
or the tides against the threads of your sheets
iizzziiiink along either side of you naked beneath me
in disbelief that beauty like this should exist.
Your scratches, so light
leaving fuzzy white trails round and
round on the calm of my back
with me joined to you there
you holding me tight and pulsing.

The *iizziiiink* marks I left on your sheets
should have been in a bed of crushed acorns,
pine-boughs and ferns,
with the sylvan folk twinkling in delight,
devas fairies sprites, whispering among themselves,
looking up, charmed by the drifting glitter of it all,
this way that way, into the black night air moon and stars.

I am not sorry, you wrote to me later,
that I have not felt this way sooner in my forty-six years,
for now I know it was always meant to be you and me.
The searching over, finally,
that empty space filled or, rather,
swells into an escalating hunger
a home to root blossoms forth
on earth (in the body) as it is in heaven (in the heart-mind).
You wrote: do you love this awakening in us,
but I already know the answer.

I believed that what you said meant what you said
and that you believed what I was was who I was,
the choosing interdependent a contract forever forth,
a surety of each other's joy in each other's
superlative yes at the mere sight of each other
everywhere drips urges to go nowhere else
but devouring here and here
uroboric the serpent regenerates itself feeding on its own tail,
infinitely sustainable, where the mystery is the deepest,
accruing another round of believing upon another of knowing.

And he *Knew* her and she *him*.
Only always compelled deeper in marriage within marriage within—
but endangered, always,
for, going incrementally further into the merging oneness,
our sustained meditation relies upon the other
who relies upon him
relying upon her.
Purity of the heart is to will one thing, Soren said.
Thus, too, endangered by the unwinding of a single strand,
the withering of a single verb,
thrown moment of distracted disbelief doubt fear what *if*—
such is the power of the word, the essentiality of the romantic narrative,
and remaining ever-devoted to and spellbound by
the shimmering glimmers it alone reveals:
"Up the curving stairs" say this and *there* we are,
"buttons pressed through" say this and *there* we are
the remembered scent of you makes me now inhale holding absorbing
only taking us further into but I already know the answer.

Build a hut in a lonely place, neither too high nor too low,
a place for worship, so say the scriptures.
First, a place: meant to be, find me here,
do you love this awakening, I already know.
Then the bodily prayers to awaken *shamanica medhra*
a thousand hours toiling into one another
those heights reached and kept, said Augustine,
were not attained by sudden flight
but they, while their companions slept,
from a certain angle into the glittery night.
The realignment of priorities,
in keeping with the purpose of life itself,
time made available hours upon
days upon weeks, years decades,
to ever deflect with each breath and fading touch
the knowledge of you back into the worship
in order to shape it as though from within and amplify its effects,
thus a knowledge is formed
that must remain secret, between us two
It lives in and passes in the rise and fall of each sigh,
fingers tracing the interior surface of your arms wrists palms fingertips
yes perfect.

High and bemused one afternoon,
we dreamed a dream of going off
blending into the trees wind streams
churning the hours the months lost
in the upward igniting bodies within bodies
each waiting for us to devote everything
for that's what it takes,
what eight hours a day are for.
One day the pineal cocoon engorges cock erect,
takes off her shirt nipples forth,
sunbursts inwardly blinding
like that first emission or menses everything suddenly
changed from one moment to the next
gone forth beyond mere fertility
flooding the full-moon suffusing everywhere
radiating into the permeating world
imbuing the living *dharma*
while all else grows hazy and remote,
we in the thick of it
the fecund mystery of incarnation
undistracted
making each other real.

In that version, we pooled our money like twelve-year olds
mischievously hiding behind the wood-pile
mixing our blood swearing oaths very serious.
Stuff with gortex got bought vaccinations air tix to Brazil
we decided would be perfect.
Unobtrusively, we arrive.
Three hours into the remote it was very hot then cold
after the second day asking around we are there.
The farmer we were told about is very old
with crushed black eyes.
He looks up at you, me,
sinks back into himself remembering something,
maybe that's why he nodded okay, come this way.
I could tell by the way your fingers teased my wrists excited
as we followed behind
this is what we have been looking for since the beginning.

Yes, some have always raced ahead
alone ominous unencumbered
the anchorites hesychasts *ardha-naris* hermits crones *vidyaharas*
swamis nuns *arhats lamas*
internalizing male and female within themselves
but their findings were hard to apply to the lives of valley-dwellers
fostering the rub with "the world."

Leaving everything behind for the greatest hunch we knew
the greatest joy, hope.
Though we have involvements other things to do places to go,
to doubt this way would be to doubt our own eyes ears
reverberations in our bodies and souls,
at some point you bet and spin.
One thing for sure, we became young very quickly in those years,
forty thirty-five thirty.
When we "walked into the forest and did not come out again,"
we smiled knew.

It was in Brazil in San Francisco in our minds
that the bursts began shooting dendrite elixirs
yeeoow into the hypoglossus *nabho mudra,*
tongues yearning for truths beyond words
searching for the gateway in out trying to find it
there *there* hidden in the soft palate the *talu nadi*
engorging reaching crawling down into slippery satiny throats
yours mine deeper entwining entering
filling our conjoined mouths become a single pulsing womb
birthing oral cathedral puberties
powerful as labor pangs stretch-marks changing everything
yours into mine into yours awakening the rosy-fingered dawn
flashing within microcosmic orbit *jing chi* swirling—

unknown bodies within unknown fractals
quivering follicles awaiting meosis
inexorably blending like potential lineages
please don't leave me,
it's beyond that, I can no longer leave you.
Source of all love songs poems prayers
vishuddha cakra awakened
the refining throat center pours forth
hushed cradle-rocking versions,
"You are my sunshine, my only…"
all the way to those starry-eyed
porch-rocking and wizened couples,
not having to even look any more
"In my life, I loved you more."

Thus, in the 5000 year history of *Sanatana Dharma*,
lives were thought to crown golden
from seventy-five years to one-hundred
in long-married pairs that slowly drifted back
further and further into Nature
vanaprasthya forest-dwellers,
wandering apart, the one eventually dying before the other,
sannyasins world-shedders,
the other living on in a kind of ecstasy
both lost from and together with,
for the veils have become gauzy now,
translucent, everything blending together,
near far then now later inside outside
yours mine birthing dying re-birthing re-dying undivided

the coursing totality a rhythm of infinite waves
wishing this way washing that,
rushing in hushing out,
upward misting of sheerest poignancy
like that first dozen roses pinkish-red petals
scattering thither by morning,
clothing strewn, champagne glasses tipped-over,
sheets turbulently entwined,
your grandparents in their mountain-top home
the Model T worn-out in the garage,
their cocktail parties you spied-on through the banisters,
they now somewhere rocking smiling rocking
eyes-closed in the same dream of memories,
the light of it all flickering,
watching us wondering bemused wistful.

The days nights and mornings were exquisite.
The rare sex centermost unfurling
from tail to crown, mysteriously intuitively.
Your back purrs should I even glance at its central groove
arising hidden and dark from the violet-tinged *trikonam*
cresting up and smoothly down into the sacral well
reaching forward between your shoulder-blades
then burying into your neck beneath the wisps of child hairs
diving into brainstem where seething rhythms of the sapient universe
flare invisibly a milky-grey conflagration of axons dendrites
filled with instinctive movements a million million combinations
to trigger hips hands lachrymose adrenaline reflexes
dormant like the birth contractions of a childless woman
till they're needed, then,

in the unswerving perfection of choiceless urgency,
it all comes forth, sweat sheens, the breath heaves
and *prana* hunts for a thousand ways
to worship existence more fully, grasping everything it finds,
hands, lips, buried anguish, lost hopes—
loins fuse, juices flow, tongues dive into throats sucking backward:
"I am the passion in beings attuned to the Final Goal."
The electrified zeal permeates the hypothalamus "little wedding chamber"
where all bio-hungers teem:
Food *now*! Labor contractions *now*!
Lactate *now*! Water, breath of life *now now*!
Sweat *now*! Shiver! Sleep, get up! Estrogen clock *now now*!
Quivering follicles give me your body your seed, your life, now,
or else it all ends with you.

But when that urgent *now* matures more fully,
mentored by the longer pineal rhythms,
patiently nourished into its puberty by rare pituitary elixirs
and incessant spinal prayers
into its transformative dark night of the soul,
no lamp for light except that one
burning in my heart (San Juan de la Cruz),
juices of creation transform into *ojas tejas retas auras*,
illuminating *citta*, further arousing *prana* awakening *Kundalini*
sending wave after wave of photovoltaic melanin endorphin
bliss currents radiating into the heavenly-winged cerebral lobes,
returning the magisterial brain
to its original mystical erogenous nature:

to *feel* it all, not via worded figurines but throbbingly
engorged and saturated
drunk with its own honeyed secretions
to become like unto gods
imbibing deep the *soma-rasa madhu* mead *amrita ambrosa*
fructified to perfection by your sultry gaze.

Whoever You Are Holding Me Now in Hand

Whoever you are holding me now in hand,
Without one thing all will be useless,
I give you fair warning before you attempt me further,
I am not what you supposed, but far different...
The way is suspicious, the results uncertain, perhaps destructive,
You would have to give up all else,
I alone would expect to be your sole and exclusive standard,
Your novitiate would even then be long and exhausting,
The whole past theory of your life and all conformity to the lives around you
would have to be abandon'd,
Therefore release me now before troubling yourself any further, let go
Your hand from my shoulders,
Put me down and depart on your way.
Or else by stealth in some wood for trial,

Or back of a rock in the open air,
(For in any roof'd room of a house I emerge not, nor in company,
And in libraries I lie as one dumb, a gawk, or unborn, or dead.)
But just possibly with you on a high hill, first watching lest any person
For miles around approach unawares,
Or possibly with you sailing at sea, or on the beach of the sea or some
quiet island,
Here to put your lips upon mine I permit you,
With the comrade's long-dwelling kiss or the new husband's kiss,
For I am the new husband and I am the comrade.
Or if you will, thrusting me beneath your clothing,
Where I may feel the throbs of your heart or rest upon your hip,
Carry me when you go forth over land or sea;
And thus touching you would I silently sleep and be carried eternally.
But these leaves conning you con at peril,
For these leaves and me you will not understand,
They will elude you at first and still more afterward,
I will certainly elude you,
Even while you should think you had unquestionably caught me, behold!
Already you see I have escaped from you.
For it is not what I have put into it that I have written this book,
Nor is it by reading it you will acquire it,
Nor do those know me best who admire me and vauntingly praise me,

Nor will the candidates for my love (unless at most a very few) prove victorious,
Nor will my poems do good only, they will do just as much evil, perhaps more,
For all is useless without that which you may have guessed at many times and not
hit, that which I hinted at;
Therefore release me and depart on your way.
Walt Whitman, 1892

Stuart Sovatsky

FOUR

Thus enlivened within, the world without blossomed.
In stores I went into the cushy stacks of color-matched
hand face bath towels sheets pillow-cases place-mats
napkins napkin-rings china sets velvet-chested silverware
all made perfect sense—
home and its making made perfect sense.
I wanted to buy it all, pick out each piece with you or surprise you.
The more perfect the hue tint shape, the more expensive—
how strange, as if there were a primordial demand-side economy
an aesthetic of Home to which craftsmen trued their wares.
I preferred the deep green-blue tinted napkins place-mats china sets
where one could not say for sure is it *green,* or is it *blue?*
From one angle in this light green but then now blue.
Enchanting, fun, our myriad laughing chatting dinner guests
will marvel feeling who we are
by our tinted goddamn place-mats wall-hangings and napkins.

Your Perfect Lips

In particular, I wanted the silverware
with knife-blades set perpendicular
to their handles allowing each to rest blade-edge down
balanced else-wise on the Scandinavian flatness
of each burnished handle because I never saw such before
because our love never happened before,
nor my life.
I dug trenches to lay perforated French drainpipe
sixty feet across my hillside gardens.
At four a.m. I carted sod home
watering it thrice a day so it would root thick greenness
where I had carved a niche eight feet wide and fifteen feet long
for our summer sleeping pavilion
we saw in some magazine and went ooh.
Stretchy black jersey sheets lingering breakfasts in the sun
the dog eating what falls to the deck
blue-green eyes to blue-green eyes.
On the chaise lounge the floor against the wall.
If we don't remember these things they will fade away.

You straightened my tie that morning just you said
to look at me a little longer. Remember?
Your precise fingers shaping the knot
centering it looking straight into my eyes
this moment is passing too quickly
chosen given over to each other
it is already passing in wider circles in other houses,
thatched-roof cabanas yurts split-levels just like us
enjoying reluctantly preparing to separate each morning it happens
you felt finally like part of the world you wrote me
the departures for offices harvests hospitals wars
factories trucks freighters not wanting to go
already feeling the missing,
and before that not wanting to get out of bed
your head on my chest breathing in breathing out perfect
maybe we will discover over the years *vi-yoga*
"the union hidden in separation" a feeling a hunch
consciousness itself has no limit.

We are one sacred household among the throngs
grihasthya sharing *oikos niemen* everything
each wave of incarnations crashes into the last
becomes a seething tangle of *karmas*
from which disentangleable we try arduously
to awaken establishing once again further down-stream
another Golden Age *Sat Yuga*
where matured gender worship reigns supreme
its invisibly ordering vibrations spreading out everywhere,
perfecting everything,
each toward its own highest maturity
swa dharma and enlightenment.

Sharing stories travels fears hopes plans
beginning detailed fantasies involving motorcycle trips
along the Slovenian Coast or Telluride,
though I felt the undertow pulling you to these places alone
a kind of freedom adventure on your own.
And your newfound novelty in being single
unaccountable in the teeming world
that beckons and gives surrogate refuge
to those outside the gender mystery
surrounded by broken halves muttering
can't be done, you'll see,
believing not a word of it themselves
privately burning inwardly with hope.

For what is love but this
uncertain flickering impermanence
embraced as it slips away
re-grasped this way then that—
through persistence romantic ardor—
surrenders to us hints of the infinite
by caring enough against all odds to worship it till,
pausing, with finger pressed to one's own lips
while preparing to express something of it again,
no next inhalation finally comes?

Against all that weight the simple pleasure
of coming home to one another the end of the day
Neil or Nora on the player eyes meeting
yes alone together home.
Names learnt work and friend's dramas followed
health conditions nieces' birthdays money woes
who said what remembering all this is devotion
is consciousness given and received,
the ultimate whether we know it or not.
These will be the concerns we have worried too much over
such is life our patch of the universe.
It vanishes except we listen care respond.

Remember that weekend at the shore
that all-night evening,
tropical fabrics you brought to cover the windows with,
the incense the candles, Joyce's *Portrait*, Calasso's *Ka*,
Wittgenstein's metre that is, is not, a metre—the standard metre
leaving all words elusive, Borges' *Circular Ruins*,
a man who dreams a man is himself another dreamer's dream
and he another? Tarot cards fun wine cheese
powdered-sugar-flecked French toast
classical guitar lingering lingering
arm-in-arm down the streets quaint with shops
a vintage clothing store the clerk is smiling at us
try it on nineteen forties furry with dangling balls perfect.
Perusing the bookstore my God on the cover of *Newsweek*
there is Christopher Reeve wheel-chaired he looks out
with watery-blue doll's eyes
hovering by a thread
staring into the far away
bearing the eternal moment
a blue breathing tube his wife firm by his side
impossible to keep looking impossible to look away
our hero now elsewhere listening to me remembering him
wishing us such closeness we should be so lucky at the end

into the next store real farm goods saddles feed-grains
fuzzy yellow-haired chicks for sale
"please do not pick up chicks"
the sign pretends not to laugh
the hip store crystals amber sachet in a carved-stone holder
it sits now by your computer
other trinkets look ooh buy not buy
who cares arm-in-arm what whither.

The next day, after the rainy windy all-night languid worship
you once wrote when will I have time to explore you
not snatches here there but long hours
and so we did the fireplace the candled bath with jets
terry-cloth robes satiny inside and everywhere I look
you are looking at me looking at you
wanting more.

Then, out of thin air perfection materialized
beach-walking, lazy-angled into each other
just happened, balancing you into me into you
heads resting mindless on shoulders yours mine
forever eyes closed in the same dark space
lost in the same smile
along the only beach in the universe
waves sliding in foamy then out, gone,
skittering birds before us gray contained and perfect.
Yes, the artsy digital photos yes, waiting for a table the crab cakes
if we keep doing this our previous lives will no longer exist.

And those long conversations sitting across from one another,
the cafes the long car rides at ease tandem,
hour-phone calls night after night talk and talk and talk.
Who could ever talk this much?
Repeating ourselves memorizing each other. Drinking it in.
You so smart behind your shyness it all came out.
More than you know.

FIVE

We were becoming friends. We liked each other.
We enjoyed hanging out, you working at your computer
with your feet arched so that your toes balanced
ruffling your hair staring into the screen.
Clickety-click on that strange keyboard
we would take sudden walks to the beach
where Japanese couples young dazzling black haired shy
and their over-laden photographers found privacy where there was none
to capture them forever smiling in color from mantles
flanked with others in black and white
with others in sepia severe and faded and others
unseen long gone wishing they were still.
Why not us too?

Why not us too run with it tripping forward more and just more?
Youme absolutely welded together you once said.
In one version that is what we did. A cascade of yeses.
Moved in within the second month
though your sister cautioned wait a while
you responded what for we just went ahead
like nothing was happening
end your lease pack up your stuff ten trips over
the boxes stacked in the garage carried in
this is your office this your den our bedroom here.
CDs condiments pans books intermixed.
Closeting our clothes together was a novel idea
but nobody's watching we liked it that way,
the blues greens blacks leathers scarves ties awash
touching each other, maybe that's why.

Your Perfect Lips

We invited our ten closest friends for dinner of quail and greens
the place-mats were a big hit the knives,
then ten of family then thirty a hundred
five a thousand, ten-thousand
looking out *sangha pradesh loka.*

A home filtered with memories
this night that the foam playground for instance,
crawling dizzy most amusing to each other what was that stuff
unable to walk to the bathroom at two a.m.
almost there tipped-over the champagne glasses
threw out a thousand empty wine bottles
from three-hundred glittering nights the guests that linger
till they finally get it, see us cooing almost embarrassing wasn't it,
okay, long drive gotta go they want some who wouldn't?
Lolling in bathrobes this happened that floss brush candles
onto the jersey stretched sleek but not as sleek as
finally quiet alone out the window
the branches are crashing into one another touching away a
wrinkle fondness into wistfulness into reveries
without middles beginnings or edges just moods drifting
pale blue yellow others beneath the horizon
of sunsets orange-tinged leaves turning
the glory of it all at the end
in the distance ahead crowning golden
we will one day vanish ethereal
into the murmuring shadows between the slender trees.

Stuart Sovatsky

We did the Slovenian Coast that first Summer
BMR's Guzzi's twisty down Italy and up amazing sunburned
what makes Italian farmers Slovenian goatherds
take us in during a sudden downpour?
—we each privately doubted would any of this happen
but real dreams always begin that way—
The oneness does.
Then the Fall Colorado wilderness on acorns pine-boughs ferns
amidst the sylvan glittering stars above
shivery then warm hot sweaty in silky down sleeping bags
condensation our very breaths on the tent's interior walls
wind-blown womb-like cathedral caves.

Wherever we went a week month three four,
we would write it all back into life read the writing to each other
to gathered friends who read us theirs,
lives weaving into weavings into *sangha* community
the dark night fire burning down in the center of a circle
toward embers of perfect couples
the children in their own circle playing with long sticks into the fire
the elders our parents their grandparents already wandering mindless
drifting heedless blending into the forests
blessing us with their rounded backs
watching through the banister atop the mountain
above the glittering wincing at the beauty of it all.
Forgive me that I linger a little longer to watch them toss the golden ball.
Forgive me that. (Nietzsche)

Remember that long *vipassana* retreat that was still to happen?
A little daunting but it takes more than heat to awaken everything.
Difficult at first to sit through knees back ankles,
but on the third day boredom shifts to nothing shifts to one long *this*
you discover the hovering for hours behind it all Mind
shimmering inner brilliance, changing your life forever.
So *that's* what it's all about!
You wanted more stunned with amazement so you went back
thirty days you sat beyond the aching in awe
barely breathing the glory of consciousness the kingdom within.
After that, the rare sex the inward upward flow
conjoined with unwavering attention
would have quickened the puberties awaiting as they are endless
blending into flesh more than a little frightening.
Singular conjoined attention excising the mind
from all that comes later.
What seems complicated
dissolved into a child fascinated by his toes.

SIX

To understand the erotic carvings on the temples at *Khajuraho*
or *Ellora* or the myriad archaic ithyphallic *Shivas,*
Krishnas cupping ithy-nippled *Radhas,*
imagine a Sistine Chapel whose high-domed ceiling
is covered with gods and goddesses as perfect lovers
in mystico-erotic embraces,
unable to get enough of themselves inside one another,
drawn by sacred forces of nature
merging the mysteries of their separate gendered bodies
into the oneness.
Halos forming around their heads pineal radiant
"with tail-feathers blazing" as Rumi sang.
Forget everything you ever heard about sex and religion
while remembering everything anew.

Apologize quickly instantly forgive waste no moments
look how beautiful you are are are.
Re-ligare, re-aligning that is re-ligion
re-and re-aligning the pairs this way that way
but according to what reference point? What standard?
It is across from each other fluctuating
and cross-fluctuating makes it interesting doesn't it?
This *Ratha Yatra*, you my standard me yours,
both in constant motion,
you the one I have waited for for so long.
Instantly attuned to you
there is no more waiting attuned to me
from this all else is calibrated
word choice actions this way that way
together physically whenever possible
touching worshipping giving up.
If we do not return, it is not some path that we will have missed,
it will be the irresistible magnificence of gender itself.

Three years into it, the heat arises relentlessly each dusk and dawn
hungry again for us to feed it playful or languid
or desperate and shivering with longings,
thus our covenant with each other another sort of pregnancy
looking to join us together in the perpetually magical time
of sun moon and stars.
Coming everywhere out of tear-ducts into the ten-thousand pores
become silky vaginas, as Ramakrishna sang.
Grimacing tongues of fire burrowing into foreheads
brows melting into brows legs braced
to catch some ache and make it soar.
Shamanica medhra this is it
asanas mudras bandhas davvening holy ghosting
transfixed in beatific stillness, willowy caresses,
weeping in loneliness overcome,
fears withered, homes found,
repose and paired, at last.

Craning your neck straining to see what is happening to you
over your shoulder another doorway opening
apana prana shooting up *asvini mudra* begins
shyly contracted frightened, coaxed,
it opens slowly like a starfish hungry
begins to quake the whole region a-swarm with answers
"between there and there lies the distance of fingers four
of which one and a half above and same below
must be left <u>alone</u> [by those unpaired
else you go mad with heat]"
now both ends of the violet-tinged ridge electrified,
(Dnyaneshwari Once again, Trans., D.S.R. Saraswati, Pune, 2002)
"one finger space that remains in the center press upon it tight"
impossible to contain like labor contractions
a juggernaut inside our bodies turbulent with unfurling secrets
"a coil of lightning a flame of fire folded
being hungry for many years and suddenly awakened
[*Kundalini*] spreads her mouth open and wide
soaring to the base of the heart she devours its longings
spreading more fire wherever there is flesh
she devours especially near the heart
devouring now every part palms soles joints nails skeleton
devouring veins breath is devoured sucking inwards
toward the source inner flashes…
I have seen the Lord and He is filled with light and sound"
what the hell have we gotten ourselves into?

Stuart Sovatsky

Madly unwinding one life, now another emerges
feeding off the last, growing into the next.
The well of elixirs *soma rasa* melanin endorphin of pineal
"moon sways and falls into the devouring mouth
spreading it everywhere the outer skin turns to powder
and a new body emerges courage without limits" (*Dnyaneshwari*)
there is another greater sky within more consciousness within
more consciousness, billowing feeding on light
on sound on breath on fire.
Take my life you said and I will take your breath away.

At fifty, you became gradually nineteen just as *Dnyaneshwar* said.
Your eyes a-glow skin wrinkles evaporating,
some minor acne emerged and faded.
Your period withered flooded withered.
Sleep expanded ten eleven twelve recovering
and waned seven five three.
Everyone around us wondered but did not know.
They talked but we told only those pairs with red-embers for eyes.
Them we told and they found their own way
running off into the distance beyond our sight
into some vanishing point beneath the horizon.

The commingling of juices absorbed into our skins membranes mouths
down our cheeks womb-folds rubbed hot and slippery
into one another. Commingling of consciousnesses
spacious myriad imaginary worlds within worlds.
Who was I who you? For those hours,
it no longer mattered who was who,
loving each other's hungers as one's own.
I looked out my eyes and was you, but you floating in us.
Happy feeling how beautiful you are from the inside,
become those freckled silky shoulders I love to caress,
wispy hairs to brush away now drift down my neck,
that smile now mine,
not the slightest worry of losing my way back,
what difference would it really make?
We would as well be each other as ourselves,
so in love in awe of each other were we.

Lost in me you were happiest all the facets gemlike
a million worded avenues alive for your inspection.
Lost in you I delighted, found repose
for you are delight you are magic.
Thus, the meditation on *citta*, the stuff of consciousness itself,
you in me me in you intensified brilliantly aglow.
When mind collapses into mind, a double infinity burgeons
uncontainable too large a library of congress
ten million books trembling with meaning
a thousand piece symphony with two-hundred flutes
three hundred strings thunderous tympani
but also kalimbas balalaikas tamburas elkhorns rainsticks
hollowed roots clanging shells.
The music of the spheres surging and angelic for our amazement.
Curled up in chairs, fire blazing, coffee swirling,
Nora Neil, we read and read them all,
turning pages lost in the mystery of it,
the wonder of it all.

Then came the coming of mouths pulsing profusely into each other
drinking madly mysterious and rare
liquid lilacs intoxicating delirious
madhu mead the honey-wine *amrita* nectar of the gods
saturating into each other's slaked thirst.
The more the drinking in the thirstier we became
drinking *drinking* drinking *drinking* getting to the last hidden dram
of floral sweetness lurking deep inside the funneled blossom
stamen pistils gold-pollen-flecked anthers,
xylem tubules and micro-tubules patiently conducting
the earthy-dew into itself and phloem nourishing back downward
into the roots, root-hairs, in dark twining intercourse with soil muck
feeling up the crystalline sand grains
nubile vibrating constantly hard wet and quivering
then back up xylem, the ruddy menstrual wine, ferric,
the sweat of us, saline licked and re-licked tenderly,
other nectars of you of me I want them all forever.

Stuart Sovatsky

The orgasms of fingertips tremble beside themselves
in syncopated delight on the backs of my hands reached out to you
they can't be restrained clutching at each other
always touching oh look! hands taking elbows shoulders waist caresses
total access taking liberties assuming *mudras*, delight-gestures,
articulating impossible languages:
This is my beloved he feels like silk she like ermine
we grip each other at the hip angling to press deeper
triggering cervical flooding. No yes, oh god!
Oceanic briny we come from those depths
until at last that unearthly throat rattle sounds
gasping hasping asping breath,
hands clutching, seizing each other stiff, birdlike,
finger talons release, gone, reversing, recedes further still,
everything fainting away, *murchaa*
in the diaphragm is sucked, *uddiyana bandha*
the upward-flying bird has grabbed the snake by the tail
carries her now in his mouth into the brainstem
where a million secrets must wait till next time.
The bird flies beyond Meru soaring out the tenth gate
leaving only stillness, the husk, behind.

Your Perfect Lips

Go, see…this is in the *Rg Veda* at the very beginning,
Garuda flies, but this flying bird is the breath
and the snake is the primordial *Kundalini*
soaring into the heaven realms
slipping by death
circular tiers of deities once human now welcome us
velvety-winged ties straightened
and into the brilliant zeal.

I think we said Oh my God at the same time then,
what was that?
It was almost funny.

The navel yearnings embedding each other with uterine hungers
back and forth up the top of our heads into the sky the ethers.
You know, storkland, first comes love then comes marriage,
then comes baby in the baby carriage.
In this version we became pregnant
that glow on your face cells bursting with Stravinski's riotous spring
hushed to a lacy whisper,
upward a vortex beckons, our new friend steps onto its edge,
slides a carnival ride downward implanting in you.
Months later she lies sleeping hushed between us become three.
Looking at each other beyond words in disbelief
that beauty like this should come forth,
deepening our roots, the fear of it all subsides.

SEVEN

Of course the orgasms of the heart.
We must begin at the edges where light-heartedness glows
but only to seduce more deeply into broken places
requiring care the old moods kindness empathy contrition forgiveness,
careful mending healing.
And then the ominous endless vow in heart's blood for real,
sworn eternal no outs, no nothing,
just the searing heat of it,
a blinding white-light pact with gender itself.
Loyalty, the strongest force in the human universe
threatened by every sort of relativity,
loyalty the last refuge
of the non-interchangeable uniqueness of each being
and the arduous distance ahead to be traversed,
one whole lifetime the measure without a second.
You can depend on me. Forever.
Who says such things?
But who would not want to?
None else than you than me, better, worse,
under the grinding wheels they leap, at once beyond.

Evenso, fear, le couer, place of courage, so fragile throbs yes, then no, then
yes…Fickle and daring, remembers every soaring moment
and seeks them evermore.
Remembers every wincing sorrow disappointment horror
and shrinks ee cummings said it best I fold close protected waiting.

But just as endlessly is the bliss remembered
and re-remembered,
looked forward to again and
created anew again, and again, this way that,
thus through our own effort faith ecstasy nearing the
vertiginous core in awestruck gendered pairs,
eye to eye into the infinitely sustainable uroboros
encircling helixes like myriad intertwining birds in flight
anther and pollen flecks by the billions
connecting sticky and pleased.

Thus, into the elder years
the advanced puberties unfold conscious and more conscious
—wisdom—enlightenment—"I see!"—forever like *this*,
equal to forever, the body fully matured
haloed pineal aglow, forged of ten-thousand nights five *ghatikas* each
equal in ardor to raising a child or two or three, the infinity of lineage,
subjugates the other priorities
in the eternal hedonism of the lascivious ascetics, *Shiva Shakti*.
Dropping everything, running off,
finding All in your blush my mind dies,
reborn conjoined zygotic, this other pregnancy
interminably throbbing with tomorrow mornings
waking in that tent eager to behold and take you me once again.

Only upward more and more suffices,
that is, nothing suffices but for a moment
—*anicca* impermanence—
another touch word thrust and another
scarf or jewel, the purpose of things,
of time itself of hands nipples standing spinal hard-ons sighs,
devotion is reality, obsession is path,
god of my god, lord of take-me,
into the heart's pubescence,
aching toward the pineal awe majesterial,
till all history, all beings,
redeemed matured none left behind.
Gargantuan stupendous insane the task
erotic crucifixion, the purpose of the universe
how could it be otherwise, everything takes everything.

And sure, we had already hurt each other
through too much or too little concern
reverberating new confusions hot reactivities,
engendering silent withdrawals, separating our powers,
weakening everything. Opening up, slowing everything down,
take the time hash it out rebuild the trust.
We are only human after all it's okay even if it isn't this is still the way.
Thus all the occult arousals are no longer surreal.
They are flowerings in weathered confusions hurts sorrows,
wind-blown, yet together still.
Even for those Marthas and Georges *Who's Afraid of Virginia Woolfs*
twisted together into the gristly strands of gender,
dawn comes once again.

There is nothing new here.
Come back, please.
It was my fault. Why did you say that that's not what I said.
Is this *samsara* strewn through with *nirvana* both at once—
the poignancy of it all?
For five years I roamed the prisons once I met a murderer
who married after twenty-five hard years the woman who met him
via letter-correspondence a pen pal as it were,
and fathers with her a son knowing full-well
he will one day look down at his shoes inhale hard
and tell that son what blood is on his hands,
thirty years ago a drug deal gone bad blam blam,
and see that son's face stunned,
the son's friends neighbors every time their eyes meet
nice guy but a murderer all the same,
"as if the shame of it must outlive him" (Kafka)
yet they conceived that son anyway,
for new life is worth it,
thus redeeming both the living and the dead.

Or those homes I have entered with bare bulbs dangling,
a can-opener for a kitchen,
making my family visits, a twenty-five year old officer of the juvenile court
amidst that stench punched-in walls federal funds dried up
no services kids huddled onto staircases giggling playfully
around needles heated spoons glue tubes up the nose
dazed tough acting children wandering into police stations
where there might be a spare dad, the lock-ups a temporary mom,
into the saliva handed loneliness behind the door
outside the guard's view forced sex acts down twelve year old legs
you think I like talking about this I believed it would all be solved by now
Vasudaiva kutumbakam and all that,
into the foster homes mental facilities closet for a bedroom,
it works I was told the men here like the food he had fifty electro-shock sessions
he told me if a child can't understand it it isn't worth knowing
his name was Wayne lobotomy scars beneath his baseball cap
that was thirty-five years ago just out of Princeton
the only thing to do or so I thought for some reason

I wanted china and silverware for the homeless Christmas dinner
not paper plastic the residence hotel smells by the boardwalk
Flander's Moldovski's Pine-sol and fermented sweat,
holiest of nectars last odors of human caring the final safety net,
life under the heap hanging on by a thread,
the dazed soldiers the hidden cost of wars gone by
in VA hospitals I saw them viciously shadow-boxing with themselves
mumbling shoulda killed 'em bastards in hell,
warehoused doped-up thorazine tongues going out and in
arms wavery pushing a laundry cart stenciled numbers on their shirts
imagine how I felt one day Canandaigua, NY VA hospital
seeing my own father wearing one swaying down a corridor
or my brother with Down's guiding a blind kid
leaning into one another holding his hand
etched in my memory their backs slumped almost one person
walking the shiny linoleum corridor florescent glare,
backwards thirty-five years before,
the spattering of swastikas in my family tree,

terminal branches replacing angled European faces who look like me
in sepia family photos how could this have happened?
The back wards I have walked,
windowless doors, the runaway shelters,
state schools with their endless rashes pneumonias,
staffed by heroes everyone.
Traveling in some village I have asked,
Why is that woman lying outside your doorway?
She is our grandmother, she is dying, *that* is what she is *doing*.

Is it a wonder that once the heart opens just a little
and you look around and feel it,
everybody just stops sinks into the please help endlessness of it,
how could anyone go on, knowing this?

But when the frenulum beneath the tongue bursts
you are snapped forward whether you want to or not,
it is hymenlike surreal inexplicable,
another virginity taken sudden hot and stinging,
the tongue freed of its slippery tether beneath.
How could a puberty be hidden in the tongue,
speaking every sort of truth imaginable,
that only one in ten-million will find?
Languages are strong, ubiquitous their hold,
forms of *life* Wittgenstein called them.
Sit still a week and you will still hear language.
Sit a year and in that silence mind into its original nature clears,
Brain escapes the semantic snare, becomes erogenous again,
another twenty, the tongue thrilled, mmmm, gets free, too.

Or drink my tongue into you where it gives up everything,
leaving a garland of skulls around my neck,
the lingual tongue engorged with endless nameless desires,
ascends swerving and questing,
the loins spinal core heart throat-pit brain-mass heat up,
fiery white searing hot, ringing with thrill.
Sword-like discernment instantaneously we feel the parsing:
Being from Words, Flesh from Logos—
the latter vows eternal to serve the former (never the reverse)
in congruence only with the highest lore of *ars erotica*
"truth is drawn from pleasure itself…"
transfiguring, masterful, singularly blissful, obliviousness to time and its limits,
elixir of life, exile of death.

These are secrets,
in some regions and times disclosure was punishable by death.
Even those who know won't confirm them.
Be less than whole-hearted in awe of the mystery,
and the chariot yaws, won't go, falters.
There are Buddha heads with tongues-to-foreheads
and no one knows why or tells.
Some cut the frenulum but that is false.
Taoists have revealed some, yes, that's true,
in English, go find them, yes that's true,
and Zen monks reverse their tongues and Christian
glossolalia tantric *nabho mudra* and *khecari mudra*
etheric space delight gestures will do just that
awaiting the lingual puberty Nature herself
draws the tongue free of its hymen,
then diving into the throat yours mine,
stirring the pineal heat, *yeow* into your mouth into mine
brain centers faint and revive into new versions of themselves
hemslves slemshelves melves slelves llvszzzz
and out the other side singing dazzling new songs
anahata-nad of holy wonder.

Stuart Sovatsky

I step outside the passion of my words
and the secrecy overwhelms me.
Should I not keep things hidden? What's the point?
It sounds crazed bizarre,
but is the averaged white world
and its favored science somehow final truth?
No, in the esoteric most hidden lurks the most real.
In the utmost secret gender worship
I create the claim that all human dilemmas wars injustice sufferings
are solved by this worship,
getting spirit further into flesh.
I hereby invent this formula:
After ten-thousand-eight hours of lingual worship
loosening the frenulum thread of karma itself,
minds meet beyond words knowing bodily, instinctively,
through senses and emotions that all beings
are as one flesh, one family.
The mental division within dissolves.
In that awakening the rest can be handled.
I hereby declare this formula Natural Law.

We cup each other's face to each other's face,
sheltering the mystery, the source of creation,
joined above below between and there,
we breathe into each other quaking ripples,
joy bursts the brain cannot take it anymore
gives up all thought, tumescent,
reverts to erogenous convolutions of infinity
where you me arise from the invisible nature of gender itself.

During this lingual pineal puberty,
the anatomy underlying speech and linguistic-knowing
outgrows the "grip" of language and its limitations
and passes through all manner of maturational longings
and sacred utterance
in which semantic purport, somatic auto-developmentalism,
and ecstatic worship converge.
Thus, the impact of the *khecari* puberty is wide-ranging.
It spiritualizes the voice, distills mental energies to a quivering stillness
revitalizes the body.

The tongue literally moves beyond linguistic-enunciation
into an esoteric vocabulary of tumescent archings
developmental delight-gestures—*mudras*—
and panlinguistic utterances,
baby-like all over again, teenaged hipster-like,
rad, gnarly new words cool-cat, with-it
in another pubescent now burst of now now now,
the tongue leans fore-and backward
in graceful or empassioned movement,
whatever theological discourse hopes to achieve,
is arrived at by purely somatic means.
Qwaali, nigune, shamanic cries, sexual moans,
labor shrieks, speaking in tongues, French kisses, cunnilingus.
The articulative mechanics of utterance
become the sonic and fleshy props
for this oral-spiritual ascent *shamanica medhra*, the next beyond.

These particular swaying arching and yearning
lingual and other bodily movements and soundings—
moreso than those of the logico-semantic ilk—
unfold now a somatic-aesthetic way to the truth.
Guided inwardly by the alluring scent glow taste
cool then heat the eternally beckoning yin-yang whorl
of the subtle-pineal's heavenly portal,
the tongue takes on this postlinguistic purpose.
The central nervous system
with its elaborately beautiful structural and energetic subtleties
becomes its own highest thought and proprioceptive feeling.
The tongue its now-silenced and prostrate devotee
licks her way toward bliss.

Comparative anatomy reveals that homosapiens
has the most elaborately ennervated tongue of all lifeforms.
That this anatomical fact should be interpreted
as an evolutionary advantage or selective adaptation
whose purpose is precise verbal articulations
is cast into the background of a far more profound bodily potential.
The unusually complex hypoglossal nerve
gives the tongue the sensitivity and muscular-articulating capacity
to stretch back toward an inner-calling,
thus stimulating the brain/mind in its maturation
beyond language-knowing
toward deeply embodied meditative *gnosis*.

Embryology as well suggests that *khecari mudra*
is part of a developmental continuity
from the earliest to this most advanced stage of bodily manifestation.
For we find that the timely secretion
of sweet-tasting mucopolysaccharides
causes the proto-tongue to lick itself away
from its embryonic contact with the hypophysis
(the rudiment of the hypothalamus and pituitary)
and out of the then-forming cranial cavity
and into the just-developing oral cavity.
It is interesting, then, to find that after years of *pranotthana,*
other sweet-tasting brain secretions (*soma, amrita*)
will again draw the tongue toward further bodily maturations
in *khecari mudra.* This time, the sweetness guides the tongue
back behind the soft palate proximal to the "little wedding chamber"
hypothalamic "appetitive-drive satiety center"
and the pituitary developmental "master gland."

During certain breathless meditative passages
that emerge during the *mudra's* hypoglossal tumescence
a psychic membrane opens certainly related to
the hypothalamic monitoring of blood oxygenation.
Through this permeable boundary between psyche and soma
an internal respiration known as *kevala kumbhaka*
begins to gasp sustenance like the first amphibious fish
who risked crawling ashore breathing no longer
through gulps of water but atmospheric oxygen.
You found a motionless way of breathing life
from the glowing *pranic* ethers of your own endless mind
interminably deep our very playground.

Stuart Sovatsky

EIGHT

In another version, none of this happens.
The chariot is running loose, fear and excitement on all sides.
Distracted from the alluring glimmers,
meant to be the one I adore welded to,
seem now chimerical imaginary a dream one night.
Unprepared for this, centripetal forces pitch abruptly,
the joyous mounting hungers clutch,
the chariot yaws, ejecting an idol,
as eight wheels on one side heave leaving the ground,
sixty-five tons bulge onto the other,
begetting splintery shudders, revealing hidden structural faults.
Yet, worse—the strange weird stillness.
Which way would it go?
False gods emerge lure and beckon,
in disbelief a path backwards surreally appears.
Before it all began returns, usurps everything
causing the chariot to rock back forth back,
once twice thrice, teetering, rolls over its
own weight and reverses into motion,
every noun traction for disagreement,
every verb a twist to get away,
memories rewritten, unbearable *adharmic*,
the chariot unhinges wheels come flying off,

candles poems scarves evaporate
arching thighs collapse, gripped wrists let go,
shirts lowered back onto raised arms
into dress and pants backwards stepping
around walking the staircase down
curved into the cold shoes
the cooing names into throats back are sucked
secret ways disappear without a trace
blackens the dimly-lit room
pulling abruptly back his hand the child was not quick enough
the velvety-winged flutters up this way that,
and vanishes.

Above the fray, *Krishna* and *Radha* whisper
"No, come, *this* is the way."
Jolted awake, suddenly everywhere is the way.
Sorry yes sorry yes do I know yes horribly yes I do too
I was remembering too yes me too I could not stop thinking.
Back again the wavery way is for real accept it,
keep coming back becoming equal to it.
Even the gods and goddess bicker disappoint so it goes,
pick up the phone, it's right there,
and it all begins anew.

NINE

Joyce has Molly say "well as well him as another"—
The mystery is right there at the end.
The choosing, the yeses, Yes the last word.
And the vortex and leaning at the edge falling over it
into the fallopian whirring slowly and the whole thing
starts up again vortex or wake the same thing from different ends
thus his other pun fin-again's-wake, his master-key to it All:
end-repeat-vortex-up, wake-down.
The Thing? The spinal channel grows
from its base *in utero* blastula become gastrula
neural groove into spine into brain terminal pineal bud
prescient always ahead of the rest,
the taste of yet-to-come.
Upward via caduseus *sushumna*
"the spinal channel where grace flows upward of its own accord,"
emerges the natural postgenital puberty age fifty,
third *ashrama vanaprasthya* forest-dwellers,
root (*mula*) and the thousand-blossoms (*sahasrara)*
connected, by one-hundred years *sannyasa,*
world-shedders, see it clearly, outside the narrowness of the day—
Sanatana Dharma, The Eternal Ordering-way.

The perineum-pineal yardstick *rta* the yard or field,
spine the stick or ruler royal way *raja* Yoga,
measure of all things sit up straight the standard metre,
zaddiks up-righteous ones:
Spinoza who saw God as Mind and Extension inner outer fields
Dionysius who gave the Divine Names
Kant who wondered beyond reason's limits
Descartes who posed the problem
Socrates awake alone and died without blinking
Plato who saw the perfect inner realm and the outer shadows
Aristotle the accountant Aquinas his deacon
Schleiermacher pleaded it's a feeling
Feuerbach saw god in humanity while
Marx implemented him *Vasudaiva kutumbakam*

Hegel looked out one eye then the other describing the wavery history
Schopenhauer soared on Eastern wings
Heidegger snitched Buddha's being-in-time
Wittgenstein awoke typing *Tractatus* in a foxhole
Derrida looked behind the curtain and found the one who speaks
Foucault meticulously fathomed shards of the broken world
Nietzsche made creation holy
The Christ loved more than we could believe
Buddha saw the Seer and dropped everything
Rumi had perfect pitch
Shiva and Uma could not stop dancing
Krishna and Radha flirted forever
Tristan and Iseult yearned into light
Romeo and Juliet ascended at sixteen
Dagwood and Blondie, Ralph and Alice made *samsara* smile
John and Yoko made Krishna and Radha envious
and it's been pretty boring ever since.

Stuart Sovatsky

TEN

A cascade of Joycean yeses
into the hands of one another
each becomes the guardian and supreme tour-guide for the other.
But well as well this one as another?
In the matching of yeses the *dharma* is sustained.
The interchangeability of lovers, however, does not prevail
over the individuality of each one
there is no interchangeability in the infinity of sequence
only an infinity of different worlds upon worlds
awaiting the willingness yes after yes.
Only singular paths unfold the Model T the foam playground,
idiosynchratic private jokes cooing names, *You.*
The worship only deepens brewing over time for those
with the same memories ends held of the same rope
engendering the twin longings,
feeding into the shared proximity
each thhiick button thhiick remembered
when where how it was slipped forth
the purpose of time itself.

Really mean it till death do us part:
Holding your wrists you writhe slightly this way then that
your outer surfaces contiguous with the invisible realms of you
giving rise to a path leading to surrenders
you squeezed my hand I give up, your hips raise to one side
you bite gently your own lower lip press your finger
as if to silence the gasp of it all fainting into yourself
into the infinity of the future uplifted into a haze
we entered the subtle realm where starry everything glows.

Each preferring to give, nothing was ever lost,
stretching ourselves thin for one another we became vast.
Easing the way for me for you as the decades wandered on
no sorrow or illness endured alone,
parents aging before us and dying, friends passing, all eventually pass.
When you squeezed my hand hard and held it there
the day I got that dreaded call, I will never forget it—
I am here, you said, I am not going anywhere,
and when my grip weakens, then my gaze upon you will lock,
when that at last should blur,
then resolute in my heart shall you remain,
your name the last sound on my lips,
your lips the last imagine in my mind…

Stuart Sovatsky

Walking down hospital corridors looking in as you pass by
you see them, one is bedside, the other lies gaunt, staring.
There I am—ten years, forty, eventually we all must say it.

As they change sheets in an empty room across the hall
you have come here the parking was difficult
you sit bedside, huge window of sky behind you,
slippery floor beneath your feet,
the dinner tray between us half-swung to the side,
half-over the bed, part-eaten dry-edged crackers,
where do hungers go when they leave you?
Leaning toward me, you trace the blue veins in my right hand
with your garden fingers the same that smoothed circles on my back.
Why do you have round doll's eyes looking at me?
Why am I staring like this?

You keep tracing looking, head poised at a slight angle,
lips pursed, just like always finding my pulse remarkable
I once touched your throat to touch your life
enchanted I wanted to spend my life near you
you cried then too do you remember?
Is it all repeating itself just like they say?
I forget what for though and eventually it all went white.
Is this what they mean? In that chair, I remember that much,
Oh, okay, suddenly blue-green wordless and beautiful
the space becomes vast.

Each begins with endless hopes joining together, and now *this*.
You stood up still leaning over me your deep neckline
I saw only your eyes this time two tunnels into the beginnings of things.
Wide-eyed atop the chariot winding streets
the one propped up on pillows the other leaning
it all had happened just the way it did
up the curving onto the cushiony mouths
devouring minds commingled breathless
but in the end even Superman just looked.
Sanatana Dharma no longer exotic, a harrowing simplicity.
It has always been *this* is *it*. What were we waiting for?

When the last throb comes, you know it. You can just barely feel it.
Voice ebbs with its ebb bb b ph hhhh total white-out.
The branches are crashing you have fallen asleep.
The tray has been taken away.

Stuart Sovatsky

An orderly comes to change the sheets
the bed is rumpled how odd to see it white and empty beneath me.
I am lost in my mind somewhere with no edges
he pulls the sheets off. Is it just a job?
Not by the look in his soul, I can't believe I just said that.
It never changes, he is thinking to himself stuffing sheets into pillowcases,
he frowns, how strange to hear him so well.
Now he is home with his wife,
I am there somehow, this is amazing,
he weeps into her breasts,
it all goes by so fast, he says,
he squeezes her hand she lowers her head onto his,
they are praying and God comes into the room.
He is just like they say, very old, watery-grey eyes
with white-hair and flowing beard,
the oldest of the old, so *that's* how He got to be God.
Now all three, orderly, wife, and God grow close
holding together, feeling it.
Behind everything everybody feels everything.

Now I am remembering in my mind's eye
the memory the vivid pictures as if yesterday of that moment
scarf trailing telling you secrets looking at your open face
the risk to to trust you with touching your throat to be a holy act.
It was July I think. You have come from that other dimly-lit room
into this one there were no English words for it,
we lived in a tent, I mean we *should have* lived in a tent,
strike while the iron, remember that saying next time
don't forget, give up everything get carried away
sell pack up, the open road before us
do you love this awakening it comes around so rarely
the feel of it a slight breeze I know you are tired but come this is the way (Rumi),
did we ever make it to the Italian coast?
The future remained to be seen
but I often remembered how your fingers delighted in holding my hand
the mere fact that I existed seemed to excite you.
I could not take my eyes off of you,
you were anxious to undress me as soon as we got home.

It was already on your mind as we walked back to my car
down that dark alley-way I made conversation you ignored it
pressing my arm quickening our pace oh I get it,
I should stop talking now I was what you wanted
though I rambled on about something you just said um hum
as you went ahead pressing buttons as I spoke babbling
um hum humoring me pulling out shirttails mine then off your own
up-stretched arms flinging it to the floor
your gaze unbroken into my eyes
you said beautiful things meant to be
absolutely welded rather be tasting,
if we forget these things they go away,
the romantic narrative is deepest truth,
one morning you burst out I adore you
that Fall we flew with the gods.

But this strange morning decades later,
as if a bird on the branch of a tree unseen,
I see you standing there below in the thick-cropped grass
in heels black stockings the fur with the balls
rows of trees far off to the sides
something slow churns through the gently crashing branches
though I cannot speak anymore I would have said
it is far more far more endless than I ever thought

BOOK TWO

Lips opening eyes into it. Again she said.
Dreams come into each other from there.
Along a thigh or arm into the sigh itself.
The writing soon ended your taste was all I could remember.
Between jasmine and spiced hashish or was it embers and ice
that caught me off-guard, spun me around
these eyes or these looking back wondering
who knows the path, really?
Who eked their way up a crag or two, really?
Who looks down upon us arm extended?
And with what message?

Into the heat of gender into the promise
the slippery home death is there—the body's.
But the mind goes on looking for you
in the next universe and the next
dizzying to see the u and s of another us
and inside them another and then another,
u's whirling down endless series of fallopian curves within curves
and s's twisting epididymis winding on down from
etheric realms, tunnels into here,
the two forever trying to become
even more Just One Us fluctuating
the one the other you me
the verb implied, that close.

BOOK THREE

A thousand years gone by,
Gender Worship reigns supreme,
Ah Foucault, we finally see how the ruses
of that little eroticism were able to rule so very long!
Simple truths you and I met again in easier times
for a long long while, enjoying and enjoying,
upward inward growing wondrously radiant with all the rest.

BOOK FOUR

After Summer comes Autumn
Winter cold and almost hopeless.
Spring, ah the fragrance of your neck.
Summer in your eyes in mine in yours.
As this Fall approaches, this time we do not forget.
Above the fray we
Krishna Radha have become.

Thirumandiram of Siddhar Thirumoolar Vol. 1

(Adapted from) B. Narajan, Translator, Babaji Kriya Yoga and Publications, Montreal, 1993

825. Pleasure of Sex Union Is Endless When Breath Savoring is the Only Way

Anointing her body with unguents diverse—Bedecking her tresses with flowers fragrant—Do you enjoy the damsel in passion's union;—If your desire becomes devotion—Prana will shoot up through the Spinal Pathway—Then your enjoyment is endless.

826. If Breath is Savored, Delicious Enjoyment Results in Sex Union

When they seek enjoyment—The breath standeth still;—The full breasted damsel and fervent male—Stand in union exalted;—As liquid silver and gold—Their passions emissions—In rapture commingleth.

827. Duration of Enjoyment Lengthens If Breath is Savored in the Copulatory Yoga That is Practiced

By the hero and the heroine—Upward they drive the coach of breath—The coach of breath—That has its wheels in regions right and left;—There they collect the waters of the heaven—And never the organs tiring know.

828. Restraint of Semen Flow Through Breath Control— This the Meaning of That Union;

When in the sex act semen flows—The yogi lets it not; but checks it—And attains within;—And a Master he then becomes.

829. Effect of Restraint of Semen Flow

He becomes master of Jnana all—He becomes master of enjoyment all—He becomes master of himself—He becomes master of senses five.

830. Sex Union Through the Pariyanga Lasts Five Ghatikas and is Bliss

This is Pariyanga Yoga (bed-yoga)—That lasts five ghatikas (2 hours)

Beyond the sixth—The damsel sleeps in the arms of the lover—In union blissful

That fills the heart—And passes description.

831. Successful Practitioners Alone Can Resort to Pariyanga

Unless it be,—He had in success practiced—The Pariyanga yoga—Of five ghatikas length—No yogi shall—A woman embrace....

834. Only Those Who Have Practiced Khecari Can Resort to Pariyanga

Lest the silvery liquid into the golden flow,—The artful goldsmith (practitioner) covered it up with yogic breath—The sparks (Kundalini) that flew traveled up by way of Spinal tube—There above,—He contained them with tongue's tip.

835. Pariyanga Yogi is Exalted

The Yogi who is in ecstastic joy—Unexcited performs this yoga with woman

Becomes radiant like the sun,—An acknowledged master in directions ten,

And of Ganas of groups eighteen.

GLOSSARY

A-dharmic disharmonious with natural, ecological forces

Ambrosia nectar of the gods

Amrita "im-mortal" nectars created within the brain centers, melatonin?

Anahata-nad endogenously-arising sounds that mature psyche and soma.

Apana prana bodily energies of excretion

Ardha-naris persons with internal balance of male and female qualities

Arhats enlightened Buddhist saints

Ars erotica pleasure-based approaches to eros

Asana Yoga postures

Ashrama life stages, child, married-parental, grandparent, great-grandparent

Asvini mudra maturating, purifying upward pull of rectal muscles

Auras the glow associated with sainthood or heroic persons

Dvaita divided

Bandha bliss-inducing, bodily-maturing and purifying erotic reflex

Bhakti devotional love

Citta the stuff of consciousness

Davvening spinal-rocking prayer form in Judaism

Dnyaneshwar Indian saint who attained complete body-mind maturation

Elan vital life-force, spirit of vitality

Ellora temple compound in India, UN designated "Treasure of the World"

Garuda giant bird in Indian mythology

Gnosis knowledge as consciousness itself, as the context for all experience

Goraksha Paddhati yogic text

gTummo/Chandal Tibetan term for mystico-erotic body heat

Grihasthya sacred family stage of life (*ashrama*)

Jagannatha Krishna as Lord of the Universe

Jing chi spiritual substrate of sexual fluids (Chinese Yoga)

Jnaneshwar see *Dnyaneshwar*

Ka the subjective feeling-nature or "who" of all beings

Karmas effects and side-effects of all actions

Kevala kumbhaka spontaneously breathless awe or serenity
Khajuraho Indian temples known for Erotico-Mystical carvings
Khecari mudra "etheric delight gesture," puberty of tongue & pineal
Kundalini (-shakti) primal maturing (force), a spiritual cognate to DNA
Lamas "saints" in Tibetan tradition
Loka realm
Lingam penis and other fleshy or energetic structures capable of tumescence
Madhu honey (mead, honey-wine)
Maha-samadhi highest cognition of the source of consciousness
Melatonin pineal secretion associated with diurnal rhythms and longevity
Moksha liberation from all immaturities
Mudra erotico-mystical delight gestures
Mula root
Murchaa swoon
Nabho mudra precursor to *khecari mudra*
Oikos neimen sharing of resources in a household, community, or world
Ojas erotico-mystical radiance of matured persons
Polypeptides mood-enhancing hypothalamic secretion
Pradesh a regional, geographic state
Prana life-force or energy
Pranotthana uplifted *prana,* via devotional or other *dharmic* activities
Quaker (ing) the erotico-mystical shaking of early American Quakers
Raja meditative or "royal" path relating to inner radiance, i.e., consciousness
Ratha Yatra Chariot Festival
Retas Erotico-mystical bodily secretions (mystical semen/ova)
Right-Left-handed paths *ars erotica* without, and with a partner, respectively
Rta "field" or the expanse of conscious awareness
Sahasrara thousand-petaled lotus, metaphor for the cerebral orgasm of mind
Samsara ever-change world wherein only highly attuned persons can be
    masterful
Sanatana Dharma eternal ways most conducive to individual/collective
    growth
Sangha local community of devotees
Sannyasin those who shed *adharmic* cultural involvements in favor of the
    dharmic
Sat Yuga Golden Age in the cosmic sequence of ages
Shaker(ing) the erotico-mystcal shaking of early American Shakers
Shamanica medhra going-beyond-the-genital-awakening

Shakti chalani movement of the feminine erotico-mystical force in the spine

Soma-rasa amrita, nectar of immortality, central object of *Rg Veda* worship

Sushumna spinal channel of deepest erotico-mystical maturation

Swa dharma developmental way of each individual being

Talu nadi erotico-mystical channel from soft palate to hypothalamus, pituitary and pineal

Tantra the weavedness of reality, and the philosophical systems that try to fathom it

Tejas erotico-mystical glow from devotional ardor

Tractatus (Logico-Philosophicus) Wittgenstein's first work

Thxiasi num Bushman term for erotico-mystical heat (*Kundalini*)

Trikonam erotico-mystical area of the perineum

Uddiyana bandha erotico-mystical reflex where the breath sucks the diaphragm upward

Urdhva-retas over-all erotico-mystical maturation within *shamanica medhra*

Uroboros mythical snake that lives by feeding upon its own tail, symbolizes infinite time

Vajroli mudra upward-sucking force in the perineum related to *urdhva-retas*

Vanaprasthya third stage of life (age 50-75), retiring grandparent-mentors

Vedas (Rg Veda) Scriptures of *Sanatana Dharma*

Vipassana focused attention that reveals the flow of moment-to-moment reality

Vishuddha chakra erotico-mystical plexus in the throat

Vi-yoga erotico-mystical unitive intimacy during times of ostensible separation

Yoni womb-spaces (vagina-uterus, or the hermetic space of mind)

Zaddick saintly or righteous person in Orthodox Judaism

Zikr (ing) a spinal-rocking Sufi prayer form

978-0-595-37587-5
0-595-37587-1

Printed in the United States
41042LVS00007B/280-510